The Book of Beetles

Matt Reher and Liam Hansen-Thiim

This is a beetle.

Power Words

How many can you read?

a	can	see
all	have	there
and	is	they
are	little	this
be	lots	you
big	of	

For more practice at this level, please visit
www.americanreadingathome.com

1-63437-583-1
978-1-63437-583-2
9 781634 375832

And this is a beetle.

All beetles have 6 legs.

All beetles have 4 wings.

All beetles have these.

Australian Christmas Beetle

Morimus Funereus

Stag Beetle

There are lots of beetles.

This is a rhinoceros.

This is a rhinoceros beetle.

Rhinoceros beetles are big.

They have lots of little hairs.

This is a leaf.

This is a leaf beetle.

Golden Flea Beetle

Scarlet Lily Beetle

Green Dock Beetle

Leaf beetles can be lots of colors.

Potato Beetle

They can have stripes.

This is a tiger.

This is a tiger beetle.

Punctured Tiger Beetle

Tiger beetles have big eyes.

They have big legs.

This is a clown.

This is a clown beetle.

Clown beetles are little.

They can be black, green, or red.

Can you see all the beetles?

Answer key:

Hercules Beetle
Musk Beetle
Green Tiger Beetle
Stag Beetle
Dung Beetle

Blue Mint Beetle
Ladybug Beetle
May Bug Beetle
Chinese Tiger Beetle
Potato Beetle
Asiatic Rhinoceros Beetle

Word Tools

Help the beetle match the color of each fruit with its word using the first letter sound!

blue

red

green

yellow

I can use the first letter sound to match the word to the picture.

flower

tiger

leaf

beetle

Beetle Facts

There are 12,000 types of beetles in the United States... and over 300,000 in the world!

Most beetles only live for a year.

Fireflies are beetles. They light up to attract potential mates.

Unlike most insects, adult beetles chew their food.

Beetles have been around for over 270 MILLION years.

Anatomy of a Beetle

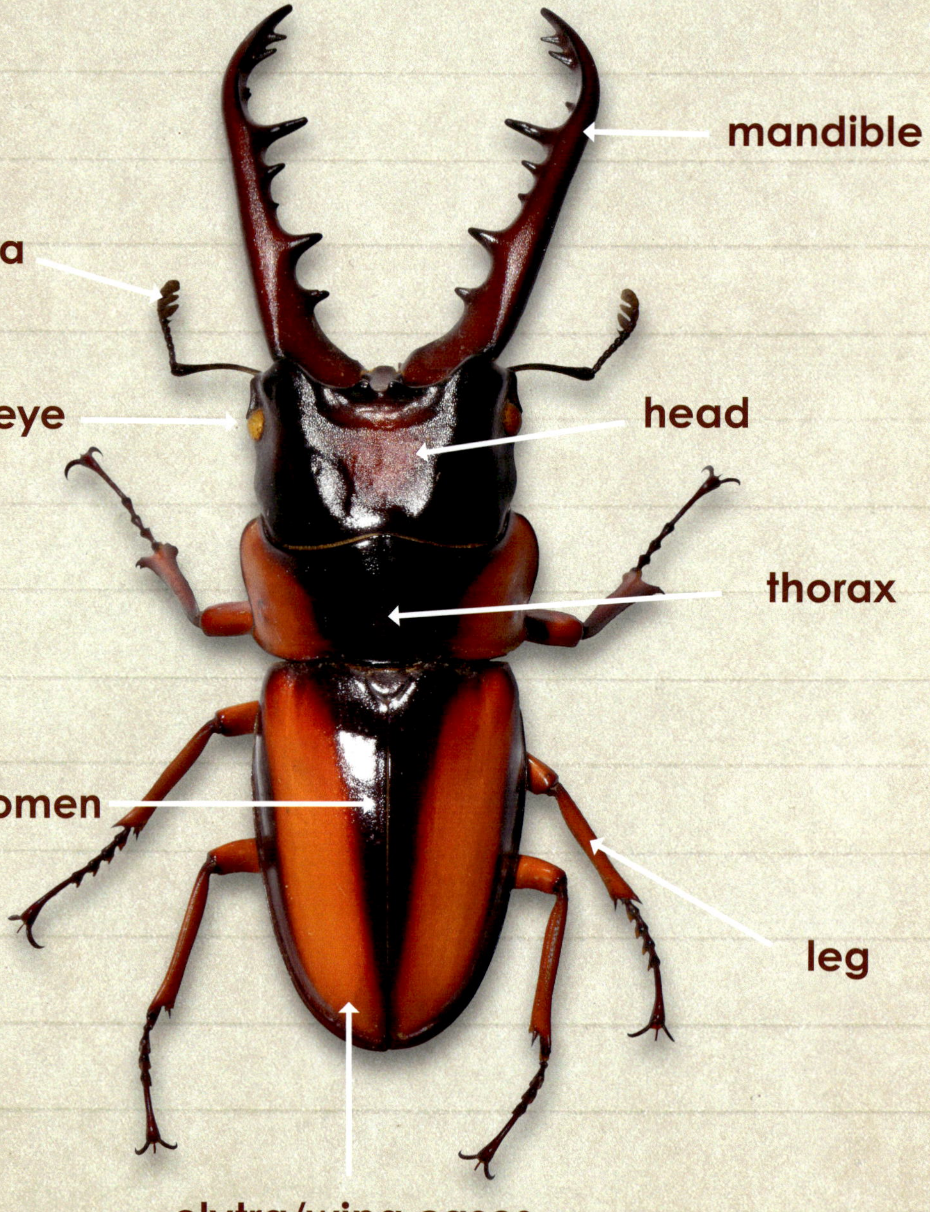